ALPHABET
COOKING CARDS

■

Cheryl A. Olmsted

FEARON TEACHER AIDS
Simon & Schuster Supplementary Education Group

For my husband, Steve, and our sons, Lance and Ian, who all fended for themselves at times so that I could write this book.

Special thanks to Jill Coudron for permission to use the names of the Alphabet Puppets.

And thanks to David Fedele, Lance Olmsted, and Crystal Forster for appearing in the cover photo.

Editor: Barbara Armentrout
Copyeditor: Diane Sovljanski
Illustration: Duane Bibby
Design: Diann Abbott
Cover Photo: Cheryl Olmsted

ISBN 0-8224-0454-0

Printed in the United States of America
1. 9 8 7 6 5 4 3 2

CONTENTS

INTRODUCTION

The recipes in this book were designed for use with Jill Coudron's *Alphabet Puppets* (Fearon Teacher Aids, 1983) in preschool, kindergarten, and primary classes. The cooking projects can, however, be presented without the puppets.

Each set of recipe cards consists of directions for preparing a single-serving snack. By working from left to right along the edge of a table or counter, the child can read each card to complete the steps in the recipe sequence.

Through these cooking experiences, the student will not only strengthen many important readiness skills, including measuring, predicting, counting, number concept, fractions, sequencing, and language development, but will also develop a keen awareness of the five senses and their functions. Additional readiness activities are provided at the end of this book, for use with the recipes and the Alphabet Puppets by Jill Coudron.

Emphasis on planning nutritious snacks and meals encourages young children to develop good eating habits early in life. Because some children may be sensitive to refined sugar, recipes requiring a sweetening agent use only pure maple syrup or raw honey.

PREPARING THE COOKING CARDS

Photocopy the recipes on white or pastel card-stock paper. (Card stock is a heavy paper that is available in office supply stores or printing shops.) Cut each page in half, and, if a corner-rounding machine is available, round the corners.

You can use water-base markers to color the title cards with the images of the alphabet animals, if you like. Do not color the direction cards, however, since color may be too distracting for some children.

Laminate all the title and direction cards. Trim the laminating film to leave about $1/4$ inch around the edges so that the cards will repel liquids. If a laminator is not available, you can use clear Con-Tact paper, but the seal around the edge may not protect the cards as well.

To keep the cards dust-free and in order, you can buy a plastic file box for 5" x 8" cards plus a set of index cards with tabs. Be sure to trim the cards to $4^1/2$" x $7^1/2$" before laminating them so that they will fit in the box. If you choose not to store the cards in a file box, you can punch a hole in the upper left-hand corner of each card and secure each recipe set with a binder ring or a brad.

EQUIPPING THE COOKING CENTER

Before cooking with the class, you should have certain equipment and utensils available or on hand.

An **oven** is required for many of the recipes. If asked ahead of time, most school cafeteria staffs are willing to preheat ovens for teachers to use. A convection oven or a toaster oven, if it is possible to acquire one for your classroom or for several classrooms, allows the children to observe changes in the foods they bake and to use their sense of smell to anticipate the treat to come!

A **refrigerator or a freezer** is required for some of the recipes. Usually, the cafeteria staff is cooperative about this, too.

A large covered **electric skillet** is much safer and easier to use for cooking foods than a skillet on a hot plate. Try to find a secondhand one, if possible, but avoid ones with peeling nonstick surfaces because they can be toxic. The nonstick skillets available today are not very expensive, and they clean up easily and quickly.

A **blender** is required for only one of the recipes. It may be most economical to bring one from home. Or you may want to buy a secondhand model if you are planning additional cooking projects for your class.

A set of cooking **utensils and supplies** is also necessary, including

a spatula,
a large spoon,
a can opener,
a sharp knife for the teacher's use,
a one-cup plastic measuring cup with incremental
    measurements on the side,
several sets of measuring spoons,
plastic tableware,
plastic bowls,
baking sheets,
a cutting board,
potholders,
toothpicks,
wax paper,
baking spray, and
an apron.

Of course, you can carry these items from home each time the class cooks, but it is easier if a permanent "kitchen" is set up in the classroom.

Since nearly every recipe requires the use of a cup, request that every child bring fifty 5-ounce **paper cups.** (You can use the request letter to parents provided at the end of this book.) These wax-coated cups can be placed directly in an electric skillet without burning. Boiling liquids in the cups will melt the wax, however, so keep that in mind if you try other recipes. Do not attempt to heat styrofoam cups in a pan or oven, because they will melt.

PREPARING FOR THE COOKING EXPERIENCE

Choose your recipe a week ahead of time so that you can begin to collect the ingredients. Send a letter to parents, asking them to provide one or more of the needed ingredients. (You can reproduce the letter provided at the end of this book.) Be sure to ask them to send the items the day before the children will cook so that you will have time to purchase or bring from home any items that might be forgotten.

On cooking day, before you start, set up all the ingredients and utensils in the cooking center. Lay out the cards so that the children will be able to walk along the table or low counter from left to right. Place the measuring cups and utensils directly on the cooking cards, and put the ingredients in plastic bowls behind the cards, with plastic knives to be used for leveling measures.

When individual servings need to be baked together, prepare 2-inch paper squares and lay out a box of toothpicks at the far right of the cooking center. Each child can write his or her name on a paper, spear it with a toothpick, and then stick it in the top of the item he or she prepared. When servings are put in paper cups to be cooked in the skillet, baked in the oven, or chilled in the refrigerator, children can write their names with pencil (not crayon) on the bottom of the cups.

GUIDING CHILDREN THROUGH THE RECIPES

You can use the Alphabet Puppet to introduce and read the recipe to the entire class. Only five or six students should be cooking at one time, however.

Give the rest of the class another activity to do until it is their turn.

Remind the children that the first step in any recipe is to wash one's hands. Then demonstrate to the whole class the entire sequence of steps, emphasizing the need to follow directions and to level off measures with a plastic knife. Children should always be supervised during the cooking experience, but lecturing should be kept to a minimum. Listen to their discussions as they work, and ask questions at appropriate times to facilitate further learning.

HEALTH AND SAFETY PRECAUTIONS

- Hands should be washed prior to cooking and should be kept away from the mouth and nose while preparing food.
- Only an adult should use electrical appliances, and they should be placed on a flat surface where no one will trip over the cord. When removing the lid from a hot pan, ask children to step back so that no one is burned by the escaping steam.
- Be sure to use only paper cups in the electric skillet. Plastic or styrofoam ones will melt.
- Children are to use only plastic knives for cutting. An adult should do any cutting that requires a sharp knife.

COOKING AT HOME

Many of the children will ask if they can have a recipe for use at home. After each cooking experience, you can duplicate the set of recipe pages and cut them in half. Then the children can color the title card, put the direction cards in the correct sequence, and finally, staple all the cards or secure them with a brad in the upper left-hand corner. Be sure to send a note to the parents explaining the use of the recipes and include the health and safety precautions. (A reproducible letter is included at the end of this book.)

Ambitious children may wish to collect all the recipes and make a cookbook with them. They can design a cookbook cover, color all the title cards, assemble the directions cards for each recipe, and then bind the cards to complete the book.

RECIPE NOTES

Multiply the single-serving ingredients by the number of children in your class to determine the total amount of ingredients needed.

Before each cooking experience, you will need to set out the recipe cards, the ingredients, and the necessary cooking implements. If additional preparation for a specific recipe is necessary, it is noted under the heading "Before-class Preparation."

APPLE ANIMAL'S APPLESAUCE

INGREDIENTS
Half an apple for each child
Cinnamon
2 T. of water for each child (1 C. water = 16 T.)
Lemon juice (to sprinkle on peeled apples)

SUPPLIES AND EQUIPMENT
Plastic bowls
Vegetable parer
Electric skillet
1 paper cup for each child
Tablespoon for measuring
Plastic knives and spoons

BEFORE-CLASS PREPARATION
Peel apples and cut them in half. Sprinkle lemon juice over apple halves so that they will not get brown.

COOKING TIME
15 minutes for one batch of apples

B. B. BUNNY'S HONEY BUTTER

INGREDIENTS
3 T. whipping cream for each child ($^1/_2$ pint whipping cream = 16 T.)
$^1/_4$ t. honey for each child (1 oz. honey = 4 t.)
Crackers or toast

SUPPLIES AND EQUIPMENT
5 or 6 baby food jars with lids
Plastic bowls
Measuring spoons: tablespoon, $^1/_4$ teaspoon
Plastic spoons and knives

BEFORE-CLASS PREPARATION
None

COOKING TIME
None

CURLY CATERPILLAR'S COLE SLAW

INGREDIENTS
2 T. slaw mix for each child (1 oz. shredded cabbage = $4^1/_2$ T.)
1 t. mayonnaise for each child (1 oz. mayonnaise = 6 t.)
$^1/_4$ t. milk for each child (1 oz. milk = 6 t.)
$^1/_4$ t. lemon juice for each child (1 oz. lemon juice = 6 t.)

SUPPLIES AND EQUIPMENT
Measuring spoons: tablespoon, teaspoon, $^1/_4$ teaspoon (2)

Plastic bowls
1 paper cup for each child
Plastic spoons and forks
Sharp knife (optional)
Juicer (optional)

BEFORE-CLASS PREPARATION

If you want to use a head of cabbage rather than slaw mix, you'll need to shred the cabbage (one 1-lb. head of cabbage yields 4$^1/_2$ C. of shredded cabbage).

If you use fresh lemon juice, you'll need to squeeze it (one lemon will yield between 1 and 3 T. of juice).

COOKING TIME

None

DITTO DOG'S DUCK DELIGHTS

INGREDIENTS

1 slice of bread for each child
1 slice of cheese for each child

EQUIPMENT AND SUPPLIES

Baking sheet
Cookie cutter in shape of duck
Oven

BEFORE-CLASS PREPARATION

Preheat oven to 350°.

COOKING TIME

About 5 minutes for each batch, or until cheese is melted.

ENOR ELEPHANT'S EASY EGGS

INGREDIENTS

1 egg for each child
1 T. milk for each child ($^1/_2$ pint milk = 16 T.)
1 T. grated cheese for each child
Salt
Oil or baking spray for skillet

EQUIPMENT AND SUPPLIES

Plastic bowls
Bowl for mixing
2 tablespoons for measuring
Electric skillet
Wooden spoon
Plastic spoons

BEFORE-CLASS PREPARATION

Grate the cheese (4 oz. of cheese will yield 16 T. of grated cheese).
Oil and preheat the skillet on low heat.

COOKING TIME

About 5 minutes for a batch of 5–6 eggs.

FRIENDLY FROG'S FANTASTIC FLAPJACKS

INGREDIENTS

2 T. whole wheat flour for each child ($^1/_2$ lb. whole wheat flour = 1$^7/_8$–2 C., or 30–32 T.)
$^1/_4$ t. baking powder for each child ($^1/_2$ oz. baking powder = 6 t.)
Salt
$^1/_4$ t. honey for each child (1 oz. honey = 4 t.)
2 T. milk for each child ($^1/_2$ pint milk = 16 T.)
1 t. beaten egg for each child (1 egg = 8–9$^1/_2$ t.)
Oil or baking spray for skillet

SUPPLIES AND EQUIPMENT

Plastic bowls
1 paper cup for each child
Measuring spoons: $^1/_4$ teaspoon (2), tablespoon, teaspoon
Plastic spoons and knives
Spatula
Electric skillet

BEFORE-CLASS PREPARATION

Beat eggs (1 medium egg will yield about 8 t. of beaten egg, and 1 large egg will yield about 9$^1/_2$ t.).
Oil and preheat the skillet on high heat.

COOKING TIME

2–4 minutes for one batch of flapjacks

GOOFY GHOST'S GRANOLA COOKIES

INGREDIENTS

1$^1/_2$ t. oil for each child (1 C. oil (or 8 oz.) = 48 t.)
1$^1/_2$ t. honey for each child 8 oz. = 48 t.
$^1/_4$ t. beaten egg for each child (1 egg = 8–9$^1/_2$ t.)
1$^1/_2$ t. chopped nuts for each child (4 oz. chopped nuts = about 36–48 t.)
1 T. whole wheat flour for each child ($^1/_2$ lb. whole wheat flour = 1$^7/_8$–2 C., or 30–32 T.)
Salt
1$^1/_3$ T. natural granola (without refined sugar—

available in natural food stores) for each child (8 oz. granola = about 40 T.)
Oil or baking spray for baking sheet

SUPPLIES AND EQUIPMENT

Plastic bowls
1 paper cup for each child
Measuring spoons: teaspoon (4), tablespoon (2), $^1/_2$ teaspoon (3), $^1/_4$ teaspoon
Plastic spoons and knives
Baking sheet
Spatula
Oven

BEFORE-CLASS PREPARATION

Preheat oven to 300°.
Beat eggs. If you have whole nuts, they will have to be chopped.

COOKING TIME

15 minutes baking time for one batch of cookies.

HAPPY HIPPO'S HONEY HERMITS

INGREDIENTS

2 T. peanut butter for each child (8 oz. peanut butter = 16 T.)
$^1/_2$ t. honey for each child (1 oz. honey = 4 t.)
$1^1/_2$ t. powdered milk for each child (1 C. powdered milk = 48 t.)
2 T. crispy rice cereal (Grainfield's or other brand sold in natural food stores) for each child (6 oz. rice cereal = about 3 C., or 48 T.)

SUPPLIES AND EQUIPMENT

Plastic bowls
1 paper cup for each child
Measuring spoons: teaspoon, tablespoon (2), $^1/_2$ teaspoon (2)
Plastic knives and spoons
Baking sheet
Refrigerator

BEFORE-CLASS PREPARATION

None

COOKING TIME

About 1 hour in refrigerator to set cookies.

INKY INCHWORM'S ICE MILK

INGREDIENTS

2 T. half-and-half for each child ($^1/_2$ pint half-and-half = 16 T.)
1 t. beaten egg for each child (1 egg = 8–9$^1/_2$ t.)
1 t. mashed banana (1 banana = about 25 t.)
$^1/_8$ t. vanilla extract for each child ($^1/_2$ oz. vanilla extract = 3 t.)

SUPPLIES AND EQUIPMENT

Plastic bowls
1 paper cup for each child
Measuring spoons: tablespoon, teaspoon (2), $^1/_8$ teaspoon
Plastic spoons
Refrigerator or freezer

BEFORE-CLASS PREPARATION

Beat the eggs. Mash the bananas just before they are to be used so that they won't turn brown.

COOKING TIME

2–3 hours in freezer to set ice milk.

JOLLY JOGGER'S CREAMY JELLO

INGREDIENTS

1 T. cold milk for each child ($^1/_2$ pint milk = 16 T.)
$^1/_2$ t. unflavored gelatine for each child ($^1/_4$ oz. envelope of gelatine = about 3 t.)
2 T. hot milk for each child ($^1/_2$ pint milk = 16 T.)
1 t. honey for each child (1 oz. honey = 4 t.)
1 T. frozen strawberries, thawed, for each child (10 oz. frozen berries = about 30 T.)

SUPPLIES AND EQUIPMENT

Plastic bowls
1 paper cup for each child
Measuring spoons: tablespoon (3), teaspoon, $^1/_2$ teaspoon
Plastic spoons and knives
Refrigerator

BEFORE-CLASS PREPARATION

Thaw the strawberries. Heat 2 T. of milk for each child.

COOKING TIME

2–3 hours in refrigerator to set jello.

KICKY KANGAROO'S KABOBS

INGREDIENTS

1 melon ball for each child
1 pitted prune for each child
1 pineapple chunk for each child

SUPPLIES AND EQUIPMENT

Plastic bowls
1 sturdy toothpick for each child
Melon-baller
Can opener (if using canned pineapple)

BEFORE-CLASS PREPARATION

Make melon balls. If you are using canned pineapple, drain it. If you are using fresh pineapple or canned slices, you'll need to cut it into chunks.

COOKING TIME

None

LOONEY LION'S LEMONADE

INGREDIENTS

$1/3$ C. water for each child
1 t. pure maple syrup for each child (1 oz. syrup = 4–5 t.)
2 t. lemon juice for each child (1 oz. lemon juice = 6 t.)
2 ice cubes for each child

SUPPLIES AND EQUIPMENT

Plastic bowls
Pitcher
1 paper cup for each child
Measuring cup
2 teaspoons for measuring

BEFORE-CLASS PREPARATION

Make enough ice cubes for the class.
If you use fresh lemon juice, you'll need to squeeze it (one lemon will yield between 1 and 3 T. of juice).

COOKING TIME

None

MERRY MOUSE'S MILKSHAKE

INGREDIENTS

3 T. milk (use lowfat to avoid the possibility of curdling) for each child (1 pint milk = 32 T.)
2 T. unsweetened pineapple juice for each child (1 pint, or 16 oz. juice = 32 T.)
1 t. pure maple syrup for each child (1 oz. syrup = 4–5 t.)
2 ice cubes for each child

SUPPLIES AND EQUIPMENT

Plastic bowls
Blender
Measuring spoons: tablespoons (2), teaspoon
1 paper cup for each child
Can opener

BEFORE-CLASS PREPARATION

Make enough ice cubes for the class.

COOKING TIME

None

NOISY NEWT'S NUTTY BREAD

INGREDIENTS

2 T. whole wheat flour for each child ($1/2$ lb. flour = $1^7/8$–2 C., or 30–32 T.)
$1/4$ t. baking powder for each child ($1/2$ oz. baking powder = 6 t.)
Salt
1 t. chopped walnuts for each child (4 oz. chopped nuts = about 36 t.)
1 t. honey for each child (1 oz. honey = 4 t.)
$1/2$ t. beaten egg for each child (1 egg = 8–$9^1/2$ t.)
1 T. milk for each child ($1/2$ pint milk = 16 T.)
$1/2$ t. oil for each child ($1/2$ C. oil = 24 t.)

SUPPLIES AND EQUIPMENT

Plastic bowls
1 paper cup for each child
Measuring spoons: tablespoon (2), teaspoon (2), $1/2$ teaspoon (2), $1/4$ teaspoon
Plastic knives and spoons
Electric skillet and lid

BEFORE-CLASS PREPARATION

Beat the eggs. Preheat skillet to 300°.

COOKING TIME

10 minutes to bake one batch of breads in covered skillet.

OH-OH OCTOPUS'S OATMEAL

INGREDIENTS

$1/3$ C. water for each child
2 T. regular oatmeal for each child (4 oz., or $1^1/4$
   C., oatmeal = 20 T.)
2 T. milk for each child ($1/2$ pint milk = 16 T.)
5 raisins for each child

SUPPLIES AND EQUIPMENT

Plastic bowls
Pitcher
Measuring cup
2 tablespoons for measuring
Electric skillet
1 paper cup for each child
Plastic spoons

BEFORE-CLASS PREPARATION

None

COOKING TIME

5 minutes for an individual portion, or for a batch
of 5–6 portions.

POLKA PIG'S PARTY PIZZA

Use X-Ray X's X Biscuits for dough recipe, plus the
following topping.

INGREDIENTS

1 T. tomato paste for each child (5 oz. tomato
   paste = 10 T.)
2 T. grated cheese for each child

SUPPLIES AND EQUIPMENT

Plastic bowls
Baking sheet
2 tablespoons for measuring
Oven

BEFORE-CLASS PREPARATION

Grate the cheese (4 oz. of cheese will yield 16 T.
of grated cheese).
Preheat the oven to 400°.

COOKING TIME

About 8–10 minutes for one batch, or until crust
browns.

QUACKY QUACKER'S QUICK QUARTERS

INGREDIENTS

1 slice of bread for each child
1 slice of cheese for each child

SUPPLIES AND EQUIPMENT

Baking sheet
Plastic knives
Oven

BEFORE-CLASS PREPARATION

None

COOKING TIME

About 3 minutes, or until cheese melts.

RACING RACCOON'S RAISIN SALAD

INGREDIENTS

1 t. mayonnaise for each child (1 oz.
   mayonnaise = 6 t.)
$1/4$ t. lemon juice for each child (1 oz. lemon
   juice = 6 t.)
$1/4$ apple for each child
1 small celery stick for each child
10 raisins for each child
1 t. chopped walnuts for each child (4 oz. chopped
   nuts = about 36 t.)

SUPPLIES AND EQUIPMENT

Plastic bowls
1 paper cup for each child
Measuring spoons: teaspoon (2), $1/4$ teaspoon
Plastic knives and spoons

BEFORE-CLASS PREPARATION

If you use fresh lemon juice, you'll need to squeeze
it (one lemon will yield between 1 and 3 T. of juice).
   Quarter apples. Wash and trim celery.

COOKING TIME

None

SPOTTY SNAKE'S EGG SALAD

INGREDIENTS

2 t. mayonnaise for each child (1 oz.
   mayonnaise = 6 t.)

¼ t. mustard for each child (1 oz. mustard = 6 t.)
1 t. milk for each child (½ pint milk = 48 t.)
1 hard-boiled egg for each child
1 t. diced celery for each child (¼ lb. diced
  celery = 30 t.)
Bread

SUPPLIES AND EQUIPMENT

Plastic bowls
1 paper cup for each child
Measuring spoons: teaspoon (3), ¼ teaspoon
Plastic knives and spoons

BEFORE-CLASS PREPARATION

Hard-boil the eggs. Dice the celery.

COOKING TIME

None

TRICKY TURKEY'S TUNA TREATS

INGREDIENTS

1 T. mayonnaise for each child (1 oz.
  mayonnaise = 2 T.)
1 t. milk for each child (1 oz. milk = 6 t.)
¼ t. lemon juice for each child (1 oz. lemon
  juice = 6 t.)
2 T. tuna for each child (6 oz. canned
  tuna = 12 T.)
1 T. diced celery for each child (¼ lb. diced
  celery = 10 T.)
1 t. chopped cashews for each child (4 oz.
  chopped nuts = about 36 t.)
Crackers

SUPPLIES AND EQUIPMENT

Plastic bowls
1 paper cup for each child
Measuring spoons: tablespoon (3), teaspoon (2),
  ¼ teaspoon
Plastic spoons and knives
Can opener

BEFORE-CLASS PREPARATION

If you use fresh lemon juice, you'll need to squeeze
it (one lemon will yield between 1 and 3 T. of juice).
Dice the celery. Open and drain tuna.

COOKING TIME

None

UGBOO'S UNPOP

INGREDIENTS

½ C. milk for each child (1 quart milk = 4 C.)
1 T. orange juice concentrate for each child (6 oz.
  juice concentrate = 12 T.)

SUPPLIES AND EQUIPMENT

Plastic bowl
Pitcher
1 paper cup for each child
Measuring cup
Tablespoon for measuring
Plastic spoons

BEFORE-CLASS PREPARATION

Defrost orange juice concentrate.

COOKING TIME

None

VAM VAMPIRE'S VANISHING VEGETABLE SOUP

INGREDIENTS

Half a potato and half a carrot, for each child
2 T. water for each child (1 C. water = 16 T.)
1 pinch of beef bouillon granules for each child

SUPPLIES AND EQUIPMENT

Plastic bowls
Plastic knives
Electric skillet
Tablespoon for measuring

BEFORE-CLASS PREPARATION

Wash and peel carrots and potatoes and cut them
in half.

COOKING TIME

About 30 minutes to simmer one batch of soup
until vegetables are tender.

WACKY WALRUS'S WASSAIL

INGREDIENTS

½ C. apple cider for each child
  (1 quart cider = 4 C.)
Ground cloves

Allspice
Nutmeg
$1/4$ t. orange concentrate for each child (6 oz. juice concentrate = 12 T.)

SUPPLIES AND EQUIPMENT

Plastic bowls
Pitcher
1 paper cup for each child
$1/4$ teaspoon for measuring
Plastic spoons
Electric skillet
Ladle

BEFORE-CLASS PREPARATION

Defrost orange juice concentrate.

COOKING TIME

About 2 minutes to warm each batch.

X-RAY X'S X BISCUITS

INGREDIENTS

$1/4$ C. flour for each child (1 lb. flour = 4 C.)
$1/4$ t. baking powder for each child ($1/2$ oz. baking powder = 6 t.)
Salt
$1/2$ t. honey for each child (1 oz. honey = 6 t.)
1 t. shortening for each child (4 oz. shortening = 24 t.)
$1^2/3$ T. milk for each child (1 pint milk = 32 T.)
Oil or baking spray for baking sheet
Flour for kneading

SUPPLIES AND EQUIPMENT

Plastic bowls
Pitcher
1 paper cup for each child
$1/4$ cup measuring cup
Measuring spoons: tablespoon, teaspoon (2), $1/2$ teaspoon, $1/4$ teaspoon
Plastic knives and spoons
Baking sheet
Oven

BEFORE-CLASS PREPARATION

If you are using solid shortening, bring it to room temperature. Oil the baking sheet. Preheat the oven to 400°. Make sure a space is clear on the table for kneading the dough.

COOKING TIME

10–12 minutes for each batch of biscuits.

YODELING YAK'S YUMMY YOGURT

INGREDIENTS

$1/4$ C. plain yogurt for each child (8 oz. yogurt = 1 C.)
1 T. pure maple syrup for each child (6 oz. syrup = 8–10 T.)
2 T. frozen strawberries for each child (10 oz. frozen berries = about 30 T.)

SUPPLIES AND EQUIPMENT

Plastic bowls
1 paper cup for each child
Measuring cup
2 tablespoons for measuring
Plastic spoons

BEFORE-CLASS PREPARATION

Thaw the strawberries.

COOKING TIME

None

ZIPPY ZEBRA'S ZAPPERS

INGREDIENTS

2 T. cream cheese for each child (3 oz. cream cheese = 6 T.)
1 t. milk for each child (1 oz. milk = 6 t.)
1 T. crushed pineapple (5 oz. crushed pineapple = 10 T.)
Celery sticks

SUPPLIES AND EQUIPMENT

Plastic bowls
1 paper cup for each child
Measuring spoons: tablespoon (2), teaspoon
Plastic spoons and knives
Can opener

BEFORE-CLASS PREPARATION

Soften cream cheese. Open and drain pineapple. Prepare celery sticks.

COOKING TIME

None

THE RECIPES

Apple Animal's Applesauce

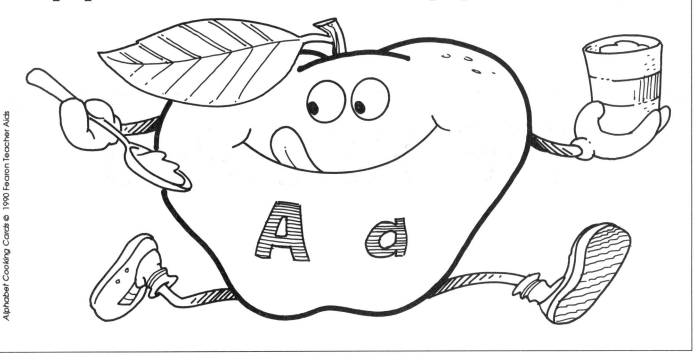

Alphabet Cooking Cards © 1990 Fearon Teacher Aids

$\frac{1}{2}$ apple

Core apple.

Alphabet Cooking Cards © 1990 Fearon Teacher Aids

Apple Animal's Applesauce

1

Place apple in skillet.

Apple Animal's Applesauce

Alphabet Cooking Cards © 1990 Fearon Teacher Aids

2

pinch of cinnamon

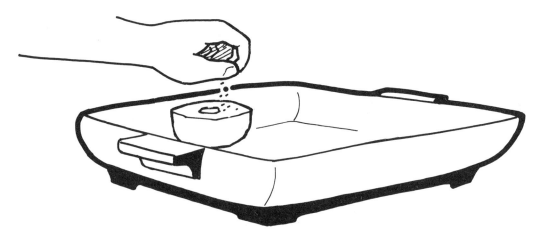

Sprinkle on apple.

Apple Animal's Applesauce

Alphabet Cooking Cards © 1990 Fearon Teacher Aids

3

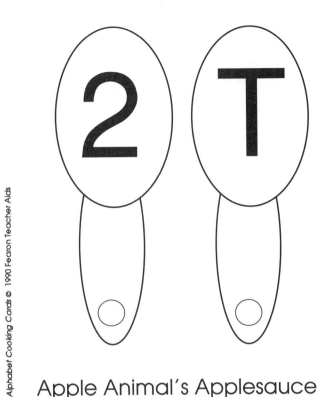 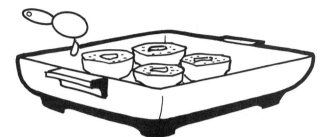

water

Pour next to apple.

Apple Animal's Applesauce

4

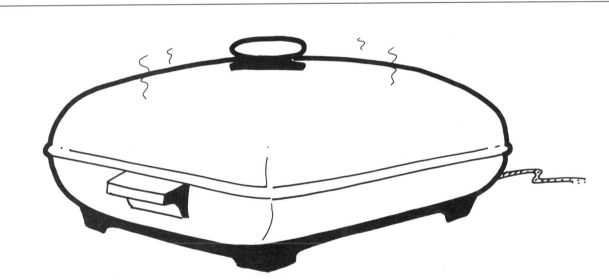

Cover skillet.
Bake until soft at 250°.

Apple Animal's Applesauce

5

Spoon apple
into cup.
Stir.

Apple Animal's Applesauce

6

B. B. Bunny's Honey Butter

3 T **whipping cream**

Pour cream into baby food jar.

Alphabet Cooking Cards © 1990 Fearon Teacher Aids

B. B. Bunny's Honey Butter

1

Cover tightly and shake until butter forms.

Alphabet Cooking Cards © 1990 Fearon Teacher Aids

B. B. Bunny's Honey Butter

2

Pour off liquid.

B. B. Bunny's Honey Butter

Alphabet Cooking Cards © 1990 Fearon Teacher Aids

3

$\frac{1}{4}$ t honey

Add to butter. Stir.

B. B. Bunny's Honey Butter

Alphabet Cooking Cards © 1990 Fearon Teacher Aids

4

Spread on crackers or toast.

B. B. Bunny's Honey Butter   5

Curly Caterpillar's Cole Slaw

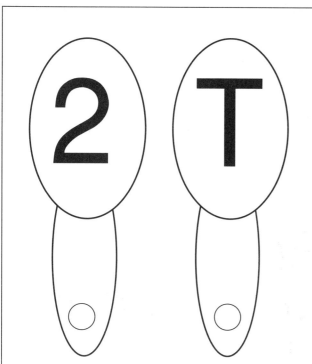

slaw mix

Pour slaw mix into cup.

Curly Caterpillar's Cole Slaw

Alphabet Cooking Cards © 1990 Fearon Teacher Aids

1

mayonnaise

Add to slaw mix.

Curly Caterpillar's Cole Slaw

Alphabet Cooking Cards © 1990 Fearon Teacher Aids

2

$\frac{1}{4}$ t milk

Add to cup.

Curly Caterpillar's Cole Slaw

3

$\frac{1}{4}$ t lemon juice

Add to cup.

Curly Caterpillar's Cole Slaw

4

Alphabet Cooking Cards © 1990 Fearon Teacher Aids

Stir.

Curly Caterpillar's Cole Slaw

5

Ditto Dog's Duck Delights

Alphabet Cooking Cards © 1990 Fearon Teacher Aids

bread slice

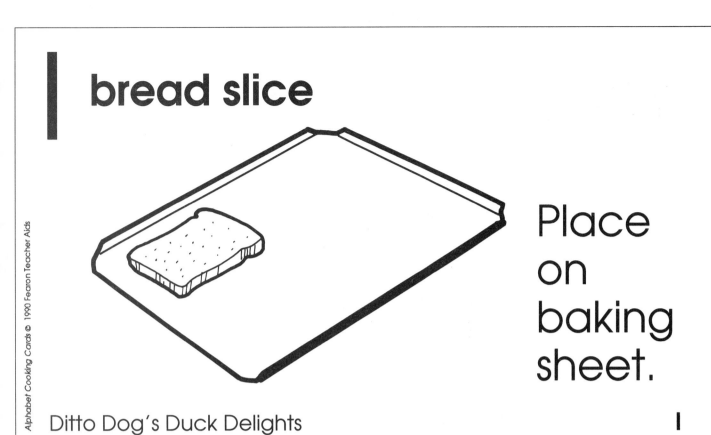

Place on baking sheet.

Ditto Dog's Duck Delights

1

cheese slice

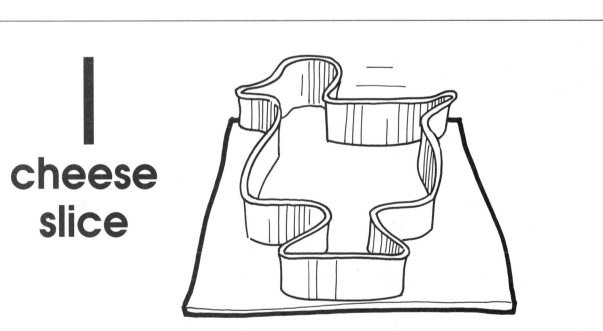

Cut cheese with cookie cutter.

Ditto Dog's Duck Delights

2

Place cheese duck on bread slice.

Ditto Dog's Duck Delights

3

Alphabet Cooking Cards © 1990 Fearon Teacher Aids

Place pan in oven and bake at 350° until cheese melts.

Ditto Dog's Duck Delights

4

Alphabet Cooking Cards © 1990 Fearon Teacher Aids

Enor Elephant's Easy Eggs

1 ⬭ egg

Crack egg over bowl.

Enor Elephant's Easy Eggs

1

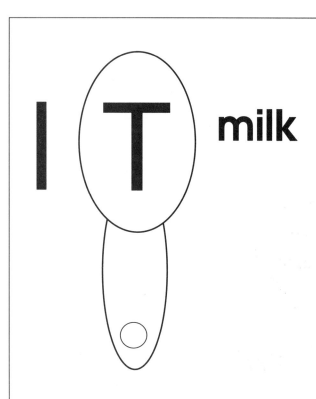 **milk**

Add to egg.

Enor Elephant's Easy Eggs

2

Alphabet Cooking Cards © 1990 Fearon Teacher Aids

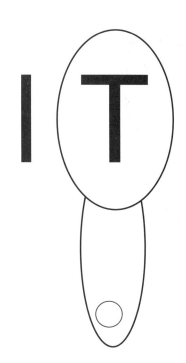 **grated cheese**

Add to bowl.

Enor Elephant's Easy Eggs

3

Alphabet Cooking Cards © 1990 Fearon Teacher Aids

pinch of salt

Add to bowl.

Stir well.

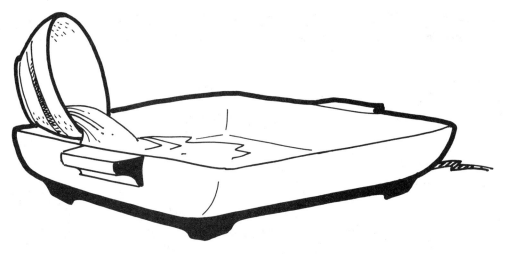

Pour into oiled skillet on low heat.

Alphabet Cooking Cards © 1990 Fearon Teacher Aids

6

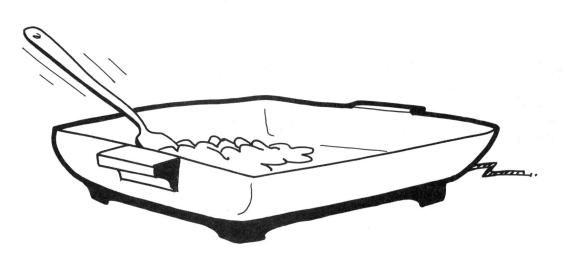

Stir the eggs slightly while they cook.

Alphabet Cooking Cards © 1990 Fearon Teacher Aids

7

Friendly Frog's Fantastic Flapjacks

2 T **whole wheat flour**

Put in cup.

Friendly Frog's Fantastic Flapjacks

I

$\frac{1}{4}$ t baking powder

Add to cup.

Friendly Frog's Fantastic Flapjacks

Alphabet Cooking Cards © 1990 Fearon Teacher Aids

2

| pinch of salt

Add to cup.   Stir.

Friendly Frog's Fantastic Flapjacks

Alphabet Cooking Cards © 1990 Fearon Teacher Aids

3

$\frac{1}{4}$ t honey

Add to cup.

Friendly Frog's Fantastic Flapjacks

4

2 T milk

Add to cup.

Friendly Frog's Fantastic Flapjacks

5

T t beaten egg

Add to cup.

Friendly Frog's Fantastic Flapjacks

Alphabet Cooking Cards © 1990 Fearon Teacher Aids

6

Stir _only_ until blended.

Friendly Frog's Fantastic Flapjacks

Alphabet Cooking Cards © 1990 Fearon Teacher Aid

7

Pour pancake batter into hot, greased skillet.

Friendly Frog's Fantastic Flapjacks

8

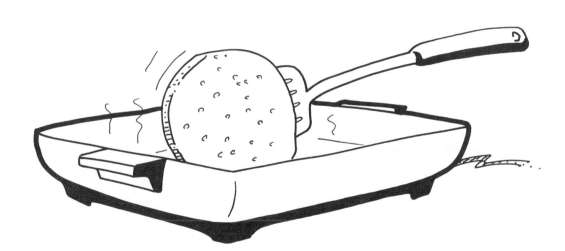

Turn when edges are brown and bubbles pop.

Friendly Frog's Fantastic Flapjacks

9

Goofy Ghost's Granola Cookies

Alphabet Cooking Cards © 1990 Fearon Teacher Aids

$$1\ \text{t} + \frac{1}{2}\ \text{t}\ \text{oil}$$

Put in cup.

Goofy Ghost's Granola Cookies

I

Alphabet Cooking Cards © 1990 Fearon Teacher Aids

1 t + $\frac{1}{2}$ t honey

Add to cup.

Goofy Ghost's Granola Cookies

2

$\frac{1}{4}$ t beaten egg

Add to cup.

Goofy Ghost's Granola Cookies

3

1 t + $\frac{1}{2}$ t chopped nuts

Add to cup.

Goofy Ghost's Granola Cookies

4

Alphabet Cooking Cards © 1990 Fearon Teacher Aids

1 T whole wheat flour

Add to cup.

Goofy Ghost's Granola Cookies

5

Alphabet Cooking Cards © 1990 Fearon Teacher Aids

pinch of salt

Add to cup.

Alphabet Cooking Cards © 1990 Fearon Teacher Aids

Goofy Ghost's Granola Cookies

6

---

1 T + 1 t natural granola

Add to cup.

Alphabet Cooking Cards © 1990 Fearon Teacher Aids

Goofy Ghost's Granola Cookies

7

Stir well.

Goofy Ghost's Granola Cookies

Alphabet Cooking Cards © 1990 Fearon Teacher Aids

8

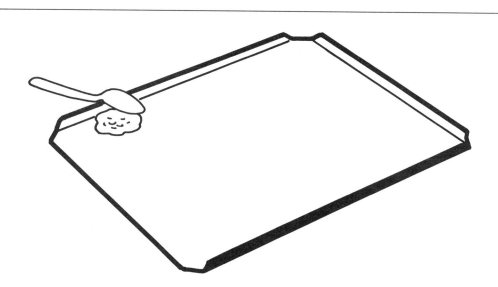

Drop dough on greased baking sheet.

Goofy Ghost's Granola Cookies

Alphabet Cooking Cards © 1990 Fearon Teacher Aids

9

Place pan in oven and bake at 300° for 15 minutes.

Goofy Ghost's Granola Cookies

10

Happy Hippo's Honey Hermits

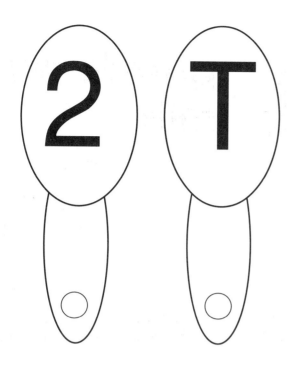

2 **T** peanut butter

Put in cup.

Happy Hippo's Honey Hermits

Alphabet Cooking Cards © 1990 Fearon Teacher Aids

1

$\frac{1}{2}$ **t** honey

Add to peanut butter.

Happy Hippo's Honey Hermits

Alphabet Cooking Cards © 1990 Fearon Teacher Aids

2

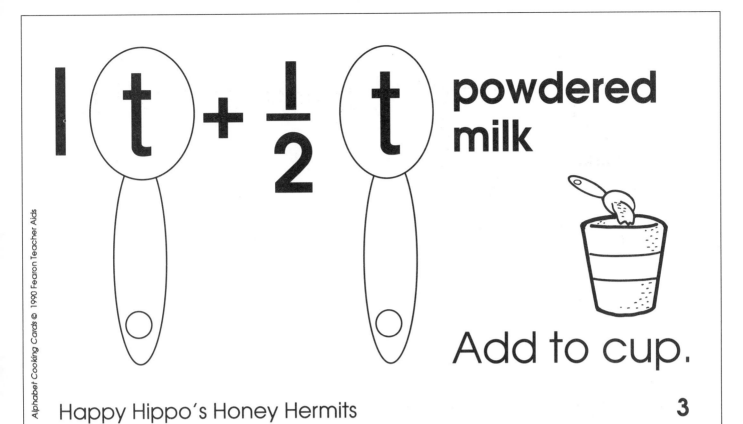

1 t + $\frac{1}{2}$ t powdered milk

Add to cup.

Happy Hippo's Honey Hermits

3

2 T crispy rice cereal

Put in cup.

Happy Hippo's Honey Hermits

4

Stir well.

Happy Hippo's Honey Hermits

5

Roll into balls.

Happy Hippo's Honey Hermits

6

Place on tray.
Refrigerate until set.

Happy Hippo's Honey Hermits

7

Inky Inchworm's Ice Milk

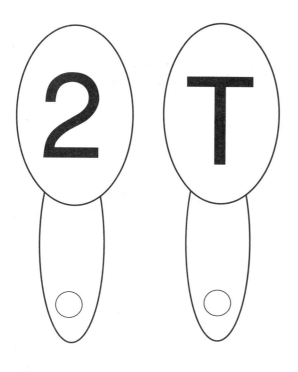

half-and-half

Pour into cup.

Inky Inchworm's Ice Milk

Alphabet Cooking Cards © 1990 Fearon Teacher Aids

1

---

beaten egg

Add to cup.

Inky Inchworm's Ice Milk

Alphabet Cooking Cards © 1990 Fearon Teacher Aids

2

1 t   mashed banana

Add to cup.

Alphabet Cooking Cards © 1990 Fearon Teacher Aids

Inky Inchworm's Ice Milk

3

$\frac{1}{8}$ t   vanilla extract

Add to cup.

Alphabet Cooking Cards © 1990 Fearon Teacher Aids

Inky Inchworm's Ice Milk

4

Stir well and freeze 'til firm.

Inky Inchworm's Ice Milk

5

Alphabet Cooking Cards © 1990 Fearon Teacher Aids

Jolly Jogger's Creamy Jello

Alphabet Cooking Cards © 1990 Fearon Teacher Aids

1 T cold milk

Pour into cup.

Alphabet Cooking Cards © 1990 Fearon Teacher Aids

Jolly Jogger's Creamy Jello

1

$\frac{1}{2}$ t unflavored gelatine

Sprinkle over milk.
Let stand 3 minutes.

Alphabet Cooking Cards © 1990 Fearon Teacher Aids

Jolly Jogger's Creamy Jello

2

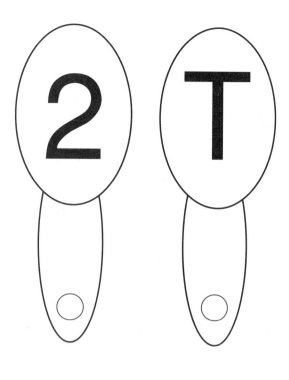

hot milk

Add to cup.

Stir until gelatine dissolves.

Jolly Jogger's Creamy Jello

3

Alphabet Cooking Cards © 1990 Fearon Teacher Aids

honey

Add to cup.

Jolly Jogger's Creamy Jello

4

Alphabet Cooking Cards © 1990 Fearon Teacher Aids

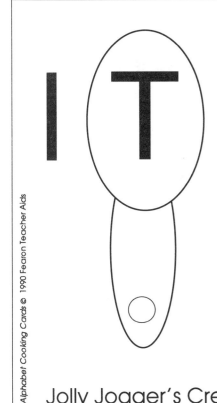 

1 T frozen strawberries, thawed

Add to cup. Stir.

Jolly Jogger's Creamy Jello

5

Refrigerate until set.

Jolly Jogger's Creamy Jello

6

Kicky Kangaroo's Kabobs

Alphabet Cooking Cards © 1990 Fearon Teacher Aids

I **melon ball**

Stick on toothpick.

Kicky Kangaroo's Kabobs

Alphabet Cooking Cards © 1990 Fearon Teacher Aids

I

prune

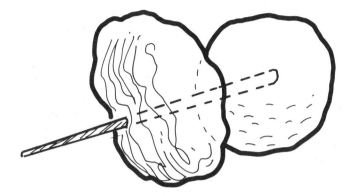

Add to toothpick.

Alphabet Cooking Cards © 1990 Fearon Teacher Aids

2

pineapple chunk

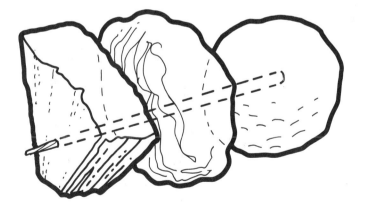

Add to toothpick.

Alphabet Cooking Cards © 1990 Fearon Teacher Aid

3

Looney Lion's Lemonade

$\dfrac{1}{3}$ C water

Pour into cup.

Looney Lion's Lemonade

I

1 t pure maple syrup

Add to water.

2

2 t lemon juice

Add to cup and stir.

3

2 ice cubes

Add to cup.

Looney Lion's Lemonade

4

Alphabet Cooking Cards © 1990 Fearon Teacher Aids

Merry Mouse's Milkshake

Alphabet Cooking Cards © 1990 Fearon Teacher Aids

3 T milk

Pour into blender.

Merry Mouse's Milkshake

1

2 T unsweetened pineapple juice

Add to blender.

Merry Mouse's Milkshake

2

1 t pure maple syrup

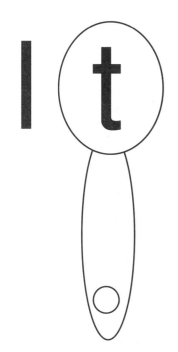

Add to blender.

Merry Mouse's Milkshake

Alphabet Cooking Cards © 1990 Fearon Teacher Aids

3

2 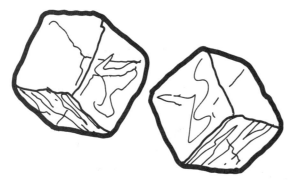 ice cubes

Add to blender.

Merry Mouse's Milkshake

Alphabet Cooking Cards © 1990 Fearon Teacher Aids

4

Blend until smooth.

Merry Mouse's Milkshake

5

Pour into cup.

Merry Mouse's Milkshake

6

Noisy Newt's Nutty Bread

Alphabet Cooking Cards © 1990 Fearon Teacher Aids

2 T whole wheat flour

Put in cup.

Noisy Newt's Nutty Bread

I

Alphabet Cooking Cards © 1990 Fearon Teacher Aids

$\frac{1}{4}$ 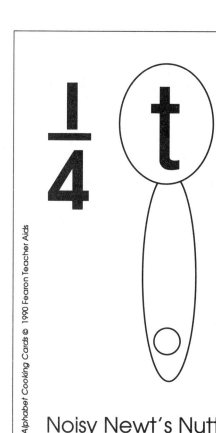 **baking powder**

Add to cup.

Noisy Newt's Nutty Bread

2

| **pinch of salt**

Add to cup.

Noisy Newt's Nutty Bread

3

I t 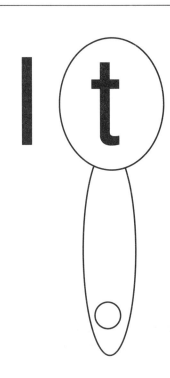 **chopped walnuts**

Add to cup and stir.

Alphabet Cooking Cards © 1990 Fearon Teacher Aids

Noisy Newt's Nutty Bread

4

I t **honey**

Add to cup.

Alphabet Cooking Cards © 1990 Fearon Teacher Aids

Noisy Newt's Nutty Bread

5

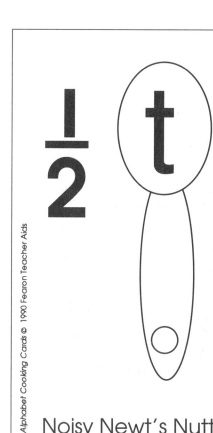

$\dfrac{1}{2}$ **t** **beaten egg**

Add to cup.

Noisy Newt's Nutty Bread

6

I T **milk**

Add to cup.

Noisy Newt's Nutty Bread

7

$\frac{1}{2}$ t oil

Add to cup. Stir.

Noisy Newt's Nutty Bread

8

Alphabet Cooking Cards © 1990 Fearon Teacher Aids

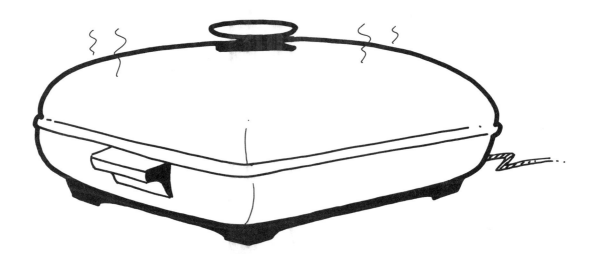

Place cup in skillet. Cover. Bake at 300° for 10 minutes.

Noisy Newt's Nutty Bread

9

Alphabet Cooking Cards © 1990 Fearon Teacher Aids

Oh-Oh Octopus's Oatmeal

$\frac{1}{3}$

C
water

Pour water
in skillet.

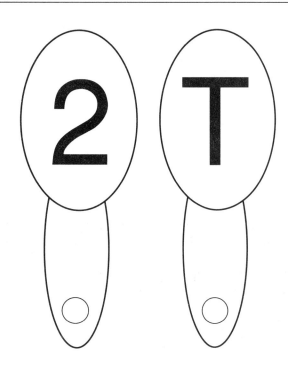 **2 T** **oatmeal**

Add to water.

Oh-Oh Octopus's Oatmeal

2

Alphabet Cooking Cards © 1990 Fearon Teacher Aids

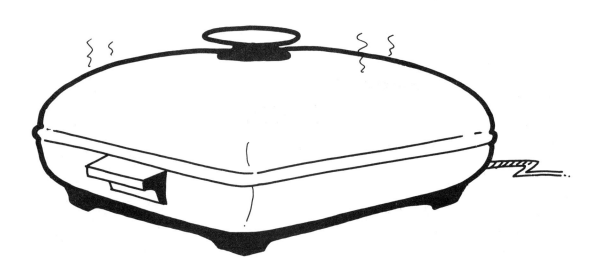

Bring to boil. Cover and cook on low for 5 minutes.

Oh-Oh Octopus's Oatmeal

3

Alphabet Cooking Cards © 1990 Fearon Teacher Aids

Spoon cooked
oatmeal into
cup.

Oh-Oh Octopus's Oatmeal

4

2 T milk

Add to cup.

Oh-Oh Octopus's Oatmeal

5

5 raisins

Add to cup.
Stir.

Oh-Oh Octopus's Oatmeal

6

Alphabet Cooking Cards © 1990 Fearon Teacher Aids

Polka Pig's Party Pizza

Alphabet Cooking Cards © 1990 Fearon Teacher Aids

X-Ray X's Biscuit dough

Flatten very thin on baking sheet.

Polka Pig's Party Pizza

1

tomato paste

Spread on biscuit dough.

Polka Pig's Party Pizza

2

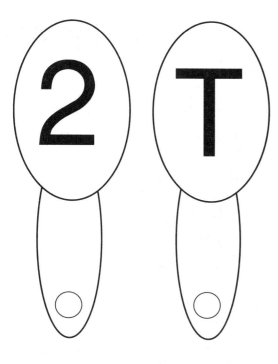

2 T **grated cheese**

Sprinkle over top.

Polka Pig's Party Pizza

Alphabet Cooking Cards © 1990 Fearon Teacher Aids

3

Place pan in oven and bake at 400° until crust browns.

Polka Pig's Party Pizza

Alphabet Cooking Cards © 1990 Fearon Teacher Aids

4

Quacky Quacker's Quick Quarters

Alphabet Cooking Cards © 1990 Fearon Teacher Aid

1 slice bread

Place on baking sheet.

Alphabet Cooking Cards © 1990 Fearon Teacher Aids

Quacky Quacker's Quick Quarters

1

| slice cheese

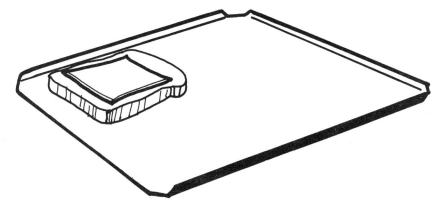

Place cheese on bread.

Quacky Quacker's Quick Quarters

2

Alphabet Cooking Cards © 1990 Fearon Teacher Aids

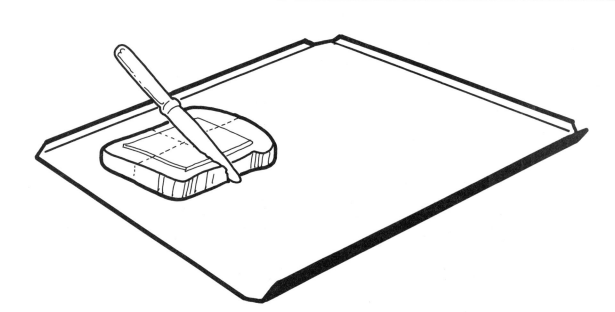

Cut bread and cheese in quarters.

Quacky Quacker's Quick Quarters

3

Alphabet Cooking Cards © 1990 Fearon Teacher Aids

<u>Teacher</u> places sheet in oven and broils until cheese melts.

Quacky Quacker's Quick Quarters

4

Racing Raccoon's Raisin Salad

1 t mayonnaise

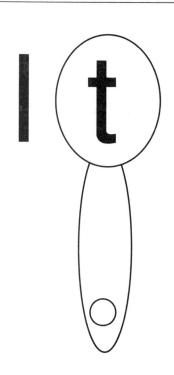

Put in cup.

Racing Raccoon's Raisin Salad

Alphabet Cooking Cards © 1990 Fearon Teacher Aids

1

$\frac{1}{4}$ **t** lemon juice

Add to mayonnaise and stir.

Racing Raccoon's Raisin Salad

Alphabet Cooking Cards © 1990 Fearon Teacher Aids

2

$\dfrac{1}{4}$ **apple**

Cut apple into small pieces and place in cup.

Racing Raccoon's Raisin Salad

3

| small celery stick

Chop celery into small pieces and add to cup.

Racing Raccoon's Raisin Salad

4

10 raisins

Add to cup.

Racing Raccoon's Raisin Salad

Alphabet Cooking Cards © 1990 Fearon Teacher Aids

5

---

1 t chopped walnuts

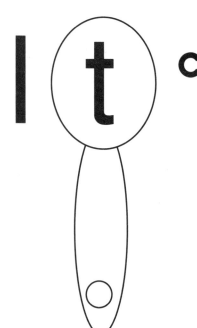 

Add to cup.

Racing Raccoon's Raisin Salad

Alphabet Cooking Cards © 1990 Fearon Teacher Aids

6

Stir.

Racing Raccoon's Raisin Salad

7

Spotty Snake's Egg Salad

2 t mayonnaise

Put in cup.

Spotty Snake's Egg Salad

Alphabet Cooking Cards © 1990 Fearon Teacher Aids

1

$\frac{1}{4}$ **t** mustard

Add to cup.

Spotty Snake's Egg Salad

Alphabet Cooking Cards © 1990 Fearon Teacher Aids

2

t milk

Add to cup and stir.

Alphabet Cooking Cards © 1990 Fearon Teacher Aids

Spotty Snake's Egg Salad

3

hard-boiled egg

Crack and peel egg.

Alphabet Cooking Cards © 1990 Fearon Teacher Aids

Spotty Snake's Egg Salad

4

Cut egg into small pieces and place in cup.

Spotty Snake's Egg Salad

Alphabet Cooking Cards © 1990 Fearon Teacher Aids

5

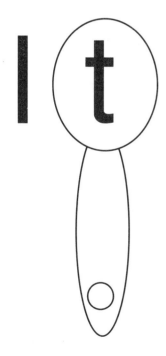 **diced celery**

Add to cup.

Spotty Snake's Egg Salad

Alphabet Cooking Cards © 1990 Fearon Teacher Aids

6

Stir and spread on bread.

Spotty Snake's Egg Salad

7

Tricky Turkey's Tuna Treats

I T **mayonnaise**

Put in cup.

Tricky Turkey's Tuna Treats

Alphabet Cooking Cards © 1990 Fearon Teacher Aids

1

I t **milk**

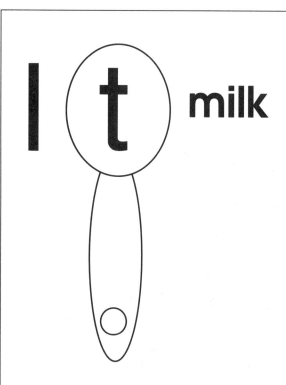

Add to cup.

Tricky Turkey's Tuna Treats

Alphabet Cooking Cards © 1990 Fearon Teacher Aids

2

$\frac{1}{4}$ t lemon juice

Add to cup and stir.

Alphabet Cooking Cards © 1990 Fearon Teacher Aids

Tricky Turkey's Tuna Treats

3

2 T tuna

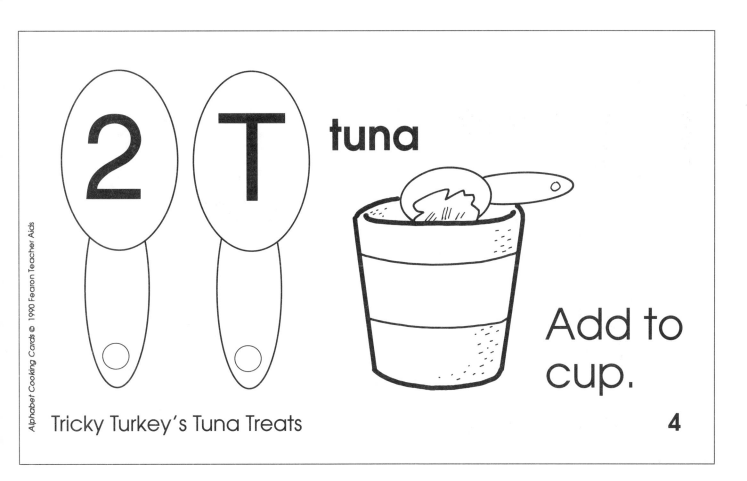

Add to cup.

Alphabet Cooking Cards © 1990 Fearon Teacher Aids

Tricky Turkey's Tuna Treats

4

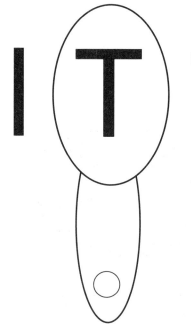 **diced celery**

Add to cup.

Tricky Turkey's Tuna Treats

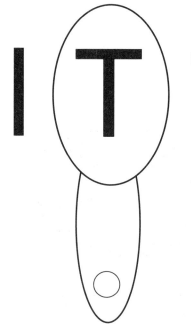 **5**

Alphabet Cooking Cards © 1990 Fearon Teacher Aids

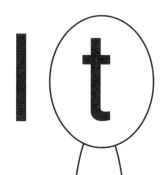 **chopped cashews**

Add to cup.

Tricky Turkey's Tuna Treats

6

Alphabet Cooking Cards © 1990 Fearon Teacher Aids

Stir and spread on crackers.

Tricky Turkey's Tuna Treats

7

Ugboo's Unpop

$\dfrac{1}{2}$ **C** milk

Pour into cup.

Ugboo's Unpop

Alphabet Cooking Cards © 1990 Fearon Teacher Aids

1

1 T **orange juice concentrate**

Add to cup.

Ugboo's Unpop

Alphabet Cooking Cards © 1990 Fearon Teacher Aids

2

Stir well.

Ugboo's Unpop

3

Vam Vampire's Vanishing Vegetable Soup

$\frac{1}{2}$ potato and
$\frac{1}{2}$ carrot

Cut into small pieces.

Vam Vampire's Vanishing Vegetable Soup

1

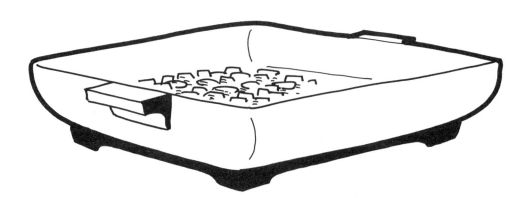

Place vegetables in electric skillet.

Vam Vampire's Vanishing Vegetable Soup

2

2 T water

Add water to skillet.

3

| pinch of beef bouillon granules

Add to skillet.

4

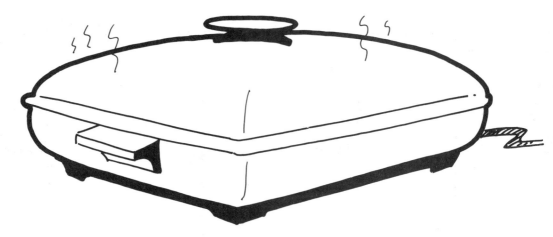

Cover skillet and simmer until vegetables are tender.

Vam Vampire's Vanishing Vegetable Soup

Alphabet Cooking Cards © 1990 Fearon Teacher Aids

5

Wacky Walrus's Wassail

Alphabet Cooking Cards © 1990 Fearon Teacher Aids

$\dfrac{1}{2}$

C apple cider

Pour into cup.

Wacky Walrus's Wassail

1

| pinch of ground cloves

Add to cup.

Wacky Walrus's Wassail

2

pinch of allspice

Add to cup.

Wacky Walrus's Wassail

Alphabet Cooking Cards © 1990 Fearon Teacher Aids

3

pinch of nutmeg

Add to cup.

Wacky Walrus's Wassail

Alphabet Cooking Cards © 1990 Fearon Teacher Aids

4

$\frac{1}{4}$ t orange juice concentrate

Add to cup.

Wacky Walrus's Wassail

5

Stir well.

Wacky Walrus's Wassail

6

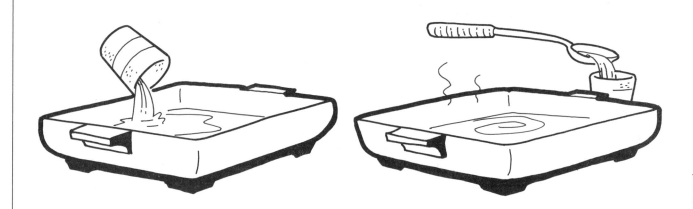

Pour into skillet. Cook until warm. Ladle into cup.

Wacky Walrus's Wassail

Alphabet Cooking Cards © 1990 Fearon Teacher Aids

X-Ray X's X Biscuits

Alphabet Cooking Cards © 1990 Fearon Teacher Aids

$\frac{1}{4}$ C **flour**

Pour into cup.

Alphabet Cooking Cards © 1990 Fearon Teacher Aids

X-Ray X's X Biscuits

2

$\frac{1}{4}$ t **baking powder**

Add to cup.

Alphabet Cooking Cards © 1990 Fearon Teacher Aids

X-Ray X's X Biscuits

2

| pinch of salt

Add to cup and stir.

X-Ray X's X Biscuits

Alphabet Cooking Cards © 1990 Fearon Teacher Aids

3

$\frac{1}{2}$ t honey

Add to cup.

X-Ray X's X Biscuits

Alphabet Cooking Cards © 1990 Fearon Teacher Aids

4

Alphabet Cooking Cards © 1990 Fearon Teacher Aids

1 t shortening

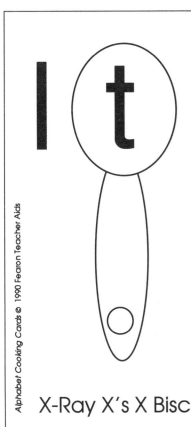

Add to cup and stir very well.

X-Ray X's X Biscuits

5

Alphabet Cooking Cards © 1990 Fearon Teacher Aids

1 T + 2 t milk

Add to cup.

X-Ray X's X Biscuits

6

Stir well.

Alphabet Cooking Cards © 1990 Fearon Teacher Aids

X-Ray X's X Biscuits

7

Knead dough on lightly floured table. Roll into 2  biscuits.

Alphabet Cooking Cards © 1990 Fearon Teacher Aids

X-Ray X's X Biscuits

8

Place on oiled baking sheet.

Place baking sheet in oven.
Bake at 400° 10–12 minutes.

Yodeling Yak's Yummy Yogurt

$\frac{1}{4}$ C

plain yogurt

Spoon
into cup.

Yodeling Yak's Yummy Yogurt

1

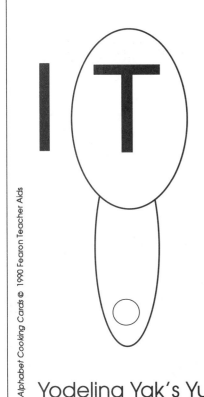

1 T pure maple syrup

Add to cup.

Alphabet Cooking Cards © 1990 Fearon Teacher Aids

Yodeling Yak's Yummy Yogurt

2

---

2 T frozen strawberries, thawed

Add to cup.

Alphabet Cooking Cards © 1990 Fearon Teacher Aids

Yodeling Yak's Yummy Yogurt

3

Stir well.

Yodeling Yak's Yummy Yogurt

4

Zippy Zebra's Zappers

2 T **cream cheese**

Put in cup.

Alphabet Cooking Cards © 1990 Fearon Teacher Aids

Zippy Zebra's Zappers

1

1 t **milk**

Add to cup.

Alphabet Cooking Cards © 1990 Fearon Teacher Aids

Zippy Zebra's Zappers

2

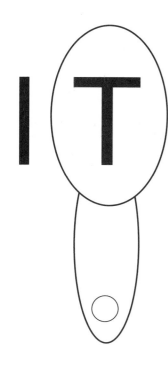

IT **crushed pineapple**

Add to cup and stir well.

Zippy Zebra's Zappers

Alphabet Cooking Cards © 1990 Fearon Teacher Aids

3

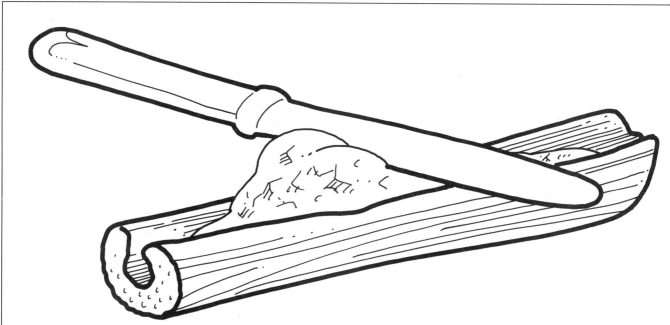

Spread on celery.

Zippy Zebra's Zappers

Alphabet Cooking Cards © 1990 Fearon Teacher Aids

4

Name _____

B.B. Bunny's Honey Butter

Color, cut, and paste to show what happened first, next, and last.

| 1 | 2 | 3 |

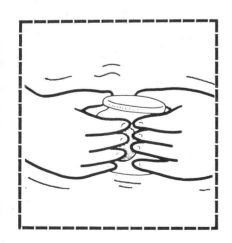

Alphabet Cooking Cards © 1990 Fearon Teacher Aids

Skill: Identify which of three activities occurs first, next, and last.

Enor's Eggs

Help Enor find the eggs.

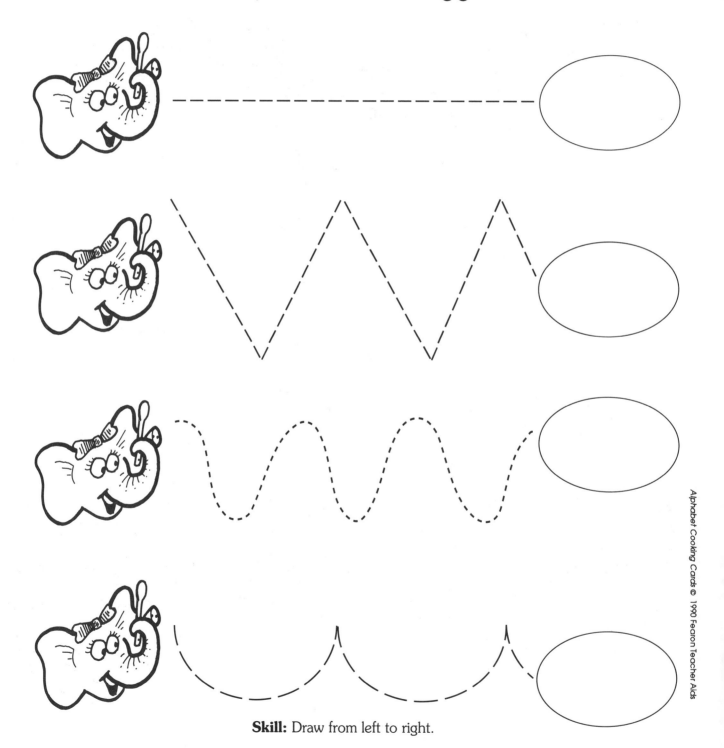

Skill: Draw from left to right.

Goofy's Granola Cookies

Color, cut, and paste Goofy's Granola Cookies.

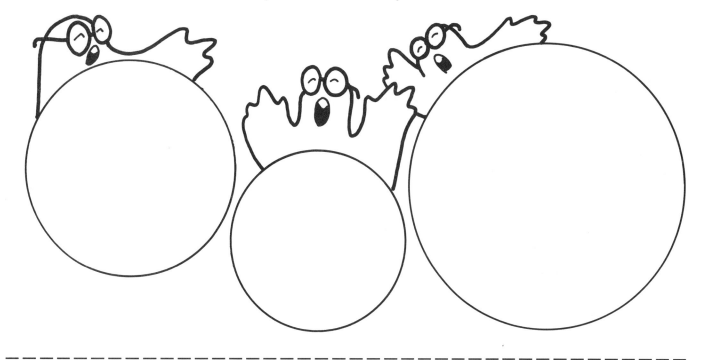

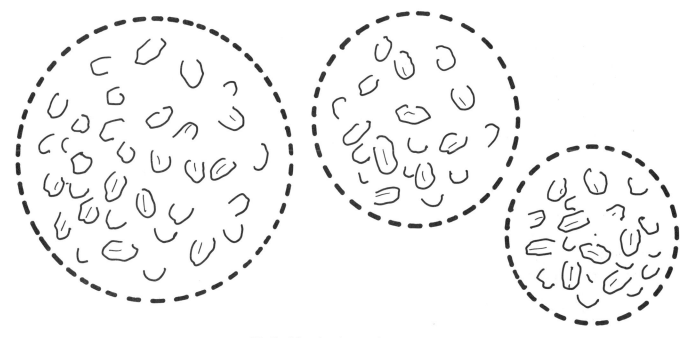

Skill: Match objects by size.

Name _____

Happy Hippo's Halves

Color one half.

Skill: Identify halves of a region and halves of a set.

108

Alphabet Cooking Cards © 1990 Fearon Teacher Aids

Kicky's Kabobs

Finish the kabob patterns.

Skill: Recognize and extend a linear pattern.

Looney's Lemonade Stand

Circle the one that holds more lemonade.

Alphabet Cooking Cards © 1990 Fearon Teacher Aids

Skill: Identify which of two containers holds more.